IMAGES
of *America*

MARION COUNTY

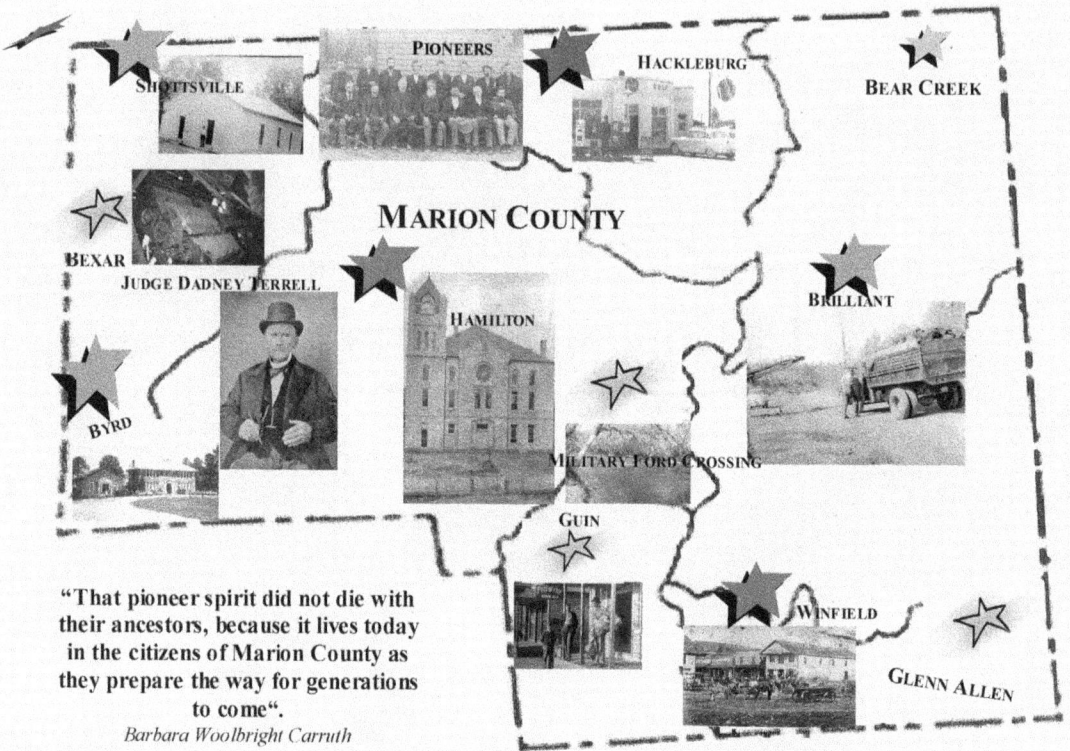

MARION COUNTY

SHOTTSVILLE

PIONEERS

HACKLEBURG

BEAR CREEK

BEXAR

JUDGE DADNEY TERRELL

HAMILTON

BRILLIANT

BYRD

MILITARY FORD CROSSING

GUIN

WINFIELD

GLENN ALLEN

"That pioneer spirit did not die with their ancestors, because it lives today in the citizens of Marion County as they prepare the way for generations to come".
Barbara Woolbright Carruth

MARION COUNTY, ALABAMA. Created in 1818, Marion County is located in northwest Alabama.

ON THE COVER: GUIN, ALABAMA. Dr. Jerry Guin donated the railroad's right-of-way to the St. Louis and San Francisco Railway, also known as the Frisco, in exchange for a stop. This stop became the town of Guin, named after the doctor who donated land for much of the town. In 1887, when the railroad was completed, a golden spike was driven in the ties near the tool house. The community had a big celebration, and Pvt. John Allen of Tupelo, Mississippi, made the dedicatory speech. After 1888, settlers began to move in.

IMAGES
of America

MARION COUNTY

Marion County Historical Society
with Barbara Woolbright Carruth

ARCADIA
PUBLISHING

Published by Arcadia Publishing
Charleston, South Carolina

Library of Congress Control Number: 2008938787

For all general information contact Arcadia Publishing at:
Telephone 843-853-2070
Fax 843-853-0044
E-mail sales@arcadiapublishing.com
For customer service and orders:
Toll-Free 1-888-313-2665

Visit us on the Internet at www.arcadiapublishing.com

CONTENTS

ACKNOWLEDGMENTS

The Marion County Historical Society and I thank everyone that helped in this endeavor: Terry Dennis with the City of Guin; Gail Spann of Main Street in Winfield; Boyd Pate and Tracy Long of Pepsi-Cola Dr. Pepper Bottling Company, Inc., of Winfield, Alabama; Gail Webb of the City of Brilliant; Brenda Burleson; Dwight Woodridge; Willie Lou Lochridge; Jean Brown; Tommy and Linda Fikes; Lynwood Clark; Tim Malone; LuAnn Harden; DeAnna Weeks; Betty Harbor; Rex Black; Mary Frances Wright; and Sara Jo Wright.

We dedicate this book to the charter members of the Marion County Historical Society. Years ago, Willie Fikes, Nannette Lawhon, Annette Sherrill, Virgil McGuire, Caroline Mixon, Pam Mixon, Gera Terrell, and Bill Mayhall came together with a desire to preserve and protect our history (Caroline Mixon and Gera Terrell are deceased, but their work is not forgotten); to the memory of Blanche Guin and the work she did to preserve our history (she too is deceased, but her work lives); and to Dr. John M. Allman III for contributions he has made to our preservation of history.

Information for the captions came from many individual sources, as well as the following books and newspaper: *The Heritage of Marion County Alabama (2000)*, *Hamilton High School: The First 100 Years* (1995), William L. White's *Self-Reliant 1900s* (1969), and the *Journal Record Newspaper Bicentennial Edition*, July 1, 1976.

All images are from the Marion County Historical Society's collection.

INTRODUCTION

Marion County covers approximately 743 square miles, lying in the northwest corner of the state of Alabama. It is bordered on the north side by Franklin County, on the east side by Winston and Walker Counties, on the south side by Fayette and Lamar Counties, and on the west side by the state of Mississippi. The county lies within the Atlantic Plain region.

Numerous tributaries of the Tombigbee River run throughout the county, as do several tributaries of the Tennessee River. The Tombigbee River is considered one of the most critical watersheds in the nation, with more than 125 species of fish, 10 of which are considered endangered. The river's many tributaries offer scenic views and recreational opportunities.

The first settlers came from Tennessee, the Carolinas, Georgia, and Virginia. It appears that the western part of the county was settled first. Early family names are Bankhead, Marchbanks, Stone, Truelove, Cantrell, McCarley, Terrell, Key, Loyd, Shotts, Pearce, Davis, Musgrove, Hamilton, White, Wiginton, Fite, Northington, Young, Weatherford, and Winstead. Marion County lies in what was once Chickasaw Indian hunting land. There are three burial mounds near the Buttahatchee River at the Military Ford crossing in Hamilton that have been reclaimed and restored in recent years by the Marion County Historical Society.

Marion County was created as one of the Alabama Territory counties on December 13, 1818, from land acquired from the Chickasaw Indians through the Treaty of 1816. The county was named in honor of Gen. Francis Marion of South Carolina, a Revolutionary War hero known as the "Swamp Fox.". In the beginning, Marion included all the territories east of the headwaters of the Tombigbee River, from its source near the Franklin County line to a point on the river in northern Clarke County. Marion then extended up the Warrior River to a point north of Tuscaloosa, then in a northwest direction to the southern boundary of Franklin County, then west of the Tombigbee River. Marion's large area included the present-day counties of Lamar, Pickens, Green, Sumter, Fayette, Walker, and Winston Counties and part of Tuscaloosa and Choctaw counties. In 1820, the legislature changed the boundaries from a line near Columbus, Mississippi, east to the Warrior River and the Jefferson County line, then north to the southeastern corner of Lawrence County. At that time, Cullman was a part of Blount County. In 1824, Marion was reduced in size by the formation of Winston County and yet again in 1866 by the formation of Jones County, which later became Lamar County.

Today Marion County brings the past alive through several festivals that include food, music, dancing, arts and crafts, and various games. One such festival is Mule Day, held annually in Winfied on the fourth Saturday in September, which draws crowds of over 25,000. Hamilton is home to the Jerry Brown Art Festival, which is heading into its seventh season in March 2009. Jerry Brown is a ninth-generation potter of hand-turned, traditional pottery. Hackleburg, birthplace of country music singer-songwriter Sonny James, celebrates Neighbor Day, and it draws a big crowd in the springtime.

As I began to write the introduction to this book, I was overwhelmed with feelings for this county called Marion and its people. I was born, grew up, and lived south of Marion County in

Lamar County, and until 1986, I knew very little of Marion or its people. My desire to engage in needful employment carried me to Marion County. After serving the fine farming community of Marion by helping to deliver farm programs from the Farm Service Agency of the United States Department of Agriculture, I retired in 2008. During those years of work, I had the privilege of getting to know people who have called Marion home for most or all of their lives. Their ancestors settled the county and endured many hardships so that others might enjoy the land today. I began to think about those pioneers and their spirit. I thought of their hard work, their dreams, and their determination. I also thought of the 22 years I had spent working in Marion County, more hours than I was home most days, and all the hardships, joys, and lessons I had learned serving these wonderful people. That pioneer spirit did not die with their ancestors; it lives today in the hard work and self-sacrifice of these citizens as they prepare the way for the generations to come. Marion County is a better place to live and work because of this spirit.

One

EARLY TOWNS
AND COMMUNITIES

COURTHOUSE IN HAMILTON.
This courthouse was built in the
very early 1900s. Today, after
renovations and add-ons gave it a
modern look much different than
this photograph, the courthouse
proudly stands, linking Hamilton
with the past. The contract to build
was issued to F. M. Dobson and
later transferred to the Alabama
Jail and Bridge Company. A special
courthouse tax was ordered by the
court to finance the building—25¢
on every $100-worth of assessed
property to be paid by landowners.

ANOTHER VIEW OF COURTHOUSE. In September 1901, the old courthouse was put up for sale, and R. E. Dunn bought it for $350. J. W. Clark was paid $19.50 to move the fireproof safe to the new courthouse. A fire insurance policy was taken out on the new courthouse with a premium of $300 for three years. For the new courthouse, W. H. White was paid $30 for 60 chairs, T. V. Bondman received $40 for the carpet, C. Northington got $1.10 for installing a window shade, and Fred Fite was allowed $5 for winding the clock for one year.

FIRST COURTHOUSE IN HAMILTON. Building of the courthouse began in 1875 and was completed in 1882 at the cost of $4,000. On a Wednesday night in late March 1887 at about 1:30 a.m., it was discovered that the courthouse in Hamilton was on fire. Before any possible effort could be made to save anything in the courthouse, it was a solid mass of flames, and it took hard fighting to keep the fire from spreading to the adjacent building. All records dating back to the time when the county was established were lost in this fire.

CIRCUS COMES TO HAMILTON. The circus came to Hamilton in 1890. Exotic animals were transported to the United States for display. The first acts in the circus were horseback riders. Soon elephants and big cats were displayed as well.

MARION COUNTY JAIL. This building was located near the present site of Hamilton Produce. Some of the early sheriffs of Marion County were Ezekiel Marchbanks, Elizah Marchbanks, Hartlett Sims, Enouch Bryant, Garret Fitzgerald, James B. Bankhead, Charles Regan, William Dennis, William T. Denny, Edwin Thomas, James McKay, William Allman, Allen Nundley, John F. Matthew, George Cannon, M. F. Atkins, Albert J. Hamilton, Lewis May, Meredith Akers, and James R. Hughes. They had offices in Pikeville.

COURTHOUSE ON FIRE. In this photograph, the courthouse appears to be on fire. Note the man on the roof spraying water into the tower and the onlookers gathered nearby. Because the structure is still standing today, it is known that the courthouse did not burn down on this date. When this building was constructed, bids were accepted and a contract given to F. M. Dobson for the sum of $21,600 to be paid in five equal installments.

DOWNTOWN GUIN, C. 1898. This view of Guin was photographed before U.S. Highway 278 was paved. According to the history of the John Allman family, Green Haley lived where Guin is today until after the Civil War. He then sold the land to John Meador, who was Judge John Dabney Terrell's stepson. Judge Terrell had considered buying it for his grandson John Mitchell Allman II. Later Dr. Jerry Guin of Tuscaloosa County purchased it from Meador.

DIRT STREETS IN GUIN. Here is a view of the old U.S. Highway 278 West toward Sulligent, before it was paved in Guin. John M. Allman II, an early resident of Guin, lived near this street and worked at J. Pearce and Company. Varina L. Pearce came to Alabama to teach and later was a clerk at J. Pearce and Company, thus meeting John. John and Varina fell in love and were married December 22, 1895.

WILLIE WIGINTON FIKES. In 1950, Willie Fikes stands in front of the courthouse where she worked from 1949 to 1959. Fikes worked for probate judge Frank Pearce. The stone courthouse was constructed in 1900 when her grandfather Thomas Wesley Wiginton was serving as county commissioner. The original law office of Ernest Baxter Fite is in the background; it was the law office of his son Ernest Rankin Fite as well. An artesian well is shown in the background.

HACKLEBURG DEPOT. Located on the Illinois Central Railroad, 17 miles northeast of Hamilton, the county seat, and 76 miles northwest of Birmingham, Hackleburg got its name because the community was overrun with a weed called hackle, which was said to be fatal to sheep.

GUIN RAILROAD WORKERS. In 1885, railroad officials came to Guin to plan for a railroad from Birmingham, Alabama, to Memphis, Tennessee. The railroad survey followed level land when possible and this brought them through Dr. Jeremiah Guin's property. He must have understood what the railroad would mean to his community because, in exchange for a right-of-way, he asked for a flag stop in Guin, making it possible for locals to travel to Birmingham and Memphis for supplies.

ARNOLD'S STORE. This photograph is of Hawks Arnold inside Arnold's Store in Hamilton.

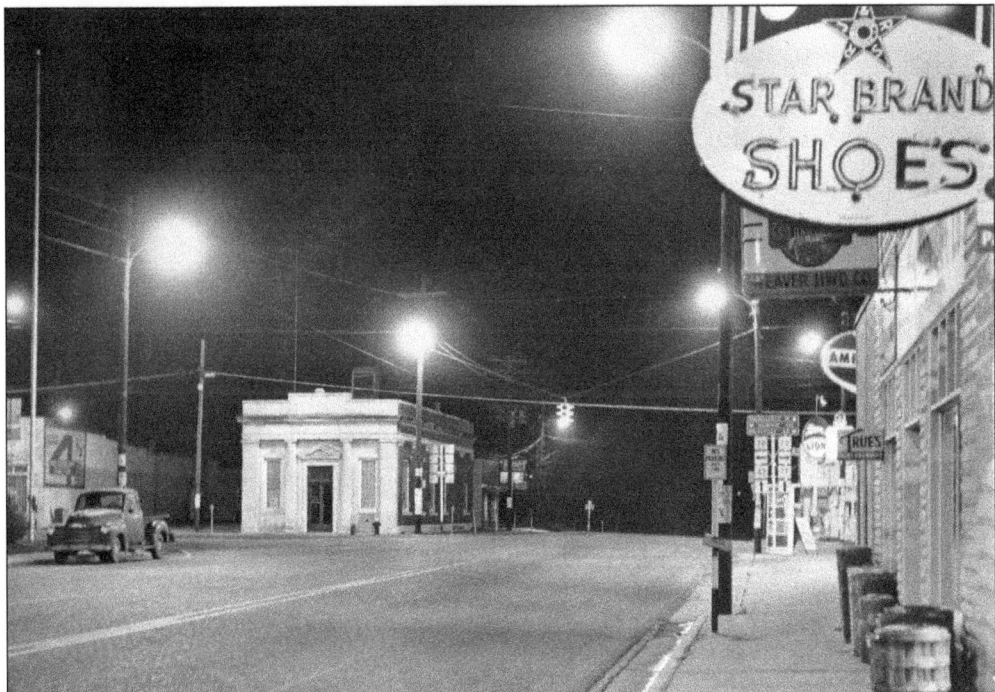

HAMILTON AT NIGHT. This is actually the second location of the Marion County Banking Company (background, left). This building still stands in downtown Hamilton and serves as the office of chiropractor Dr. Anthony Ambrosino.

HACKLEBURG, SMALL TOWN IN MARION COUNTY. Pictured is an unidentified woman in front of the movie theater in Hackleburg, Alabama. Hackleburg was the birthplace of country singer-songwriter Sonny James, who was born Jimmy Loden, son of Archie and Della Burleson Loden. Sonny's parents owned and operated a 300-acre farm about 6 miles outside of town. Their farm supported three tenant families who worked together using teams of horses and mules to raise enough cotton, corn, and hay to see them through each season.

FOWLER GROCERY. This photograph was taken inside Fowler's Grocery in Hackleburg. Ed Fowler came to Hackleburg as a young man, working in a store as a clerk. He later owned and worked in Fowler's Grocery, and served customers in this small town for 50 years. Max Isom, Joyce Vandiver, and Ellis Stidham are among Fowler's list of employees through the years. Fowler is remembered as one who gave back to his community.

BRIDGEWORK NEAR GUIN. Unidentified men are working on a bridge near Guin. In the early days of building roads and bridge work, the county used volunteer workers. In some areas, men were obligated to work a number of days each year on the county roads.

CROWD AT GUIN DEPOT. Friends and relatives gathered at the town's depot to see local men leave for World War I service in 1916 or 1917. Between Louis and Carlos May is an unidentified Baxter boy, and Middleton Sizemore is the gentleman with his back turned behind and to the left of the man labeled "Fred."

HACKLEBURG. Hackleburg is a small town at the intersection of the Russellville Pike, the old Allen's Factory, and the Iuka stagecoach road. Native Americans were numerous in this area when the first white settlers arrived, and carvings made by them on stones and trees still existed in the 1930s. Hackleburg was hunting ground for the Chickasaw Indians, and arrowheads and places where corn was ground have been found.

HACKLEBURG DOWNTOWN. The name was given to the town by a Tennessee sheep drover who, to his sorrow, lost several of his animals when they were driven into a patch of the hackle weed. According to reports of the incident, the weed ruined the fleece and caused the death of many of the sheep. In his wrath, the Tennessean gave the name of the weed to the settlement, and it has clung to it ever since.

GULF STATION. Pictured above is Jack Ridings, the owner of this service station. Gulf gas stations evolved from being "filling" stations in the 1920s and 1930s to "service" stations, where owners were able to stock their shelves with various goods and generate other income instead of making money just from gas. The stations were soon updated to include restrooms and service areas.

BUTTAHATCHEE RIVER. Three Native American burial mounds have been preserved at the Military Ford crossing of the Buttahatchee River in Hamilton. The name Buttahatchee is believed to be from the Choctaw Indian tongue and is interpreted as "Sumac River." The river rises in northwestern Winston County, Alabama, and flows generally westward through Marion County.

WIGINTON PAPER IN HACKLEBURG. Wiginton Paper Products, Inc., began operation in June 1968 in the old Wiginton School building. Operations continued in this building until the early 1980s when fire destroyed the structure. At that time, the operations were moved to their present location on Main Street. Pictured is Rex Williford, founder of Wiginton Paper Products, who passed away in 1988. Since that time, his son Warren Williford has continued the business, serving as president.

HACKLEBURG SERVICE STATION. Pictured here is Woods Howell in front of his service station in Hackleburg. In 1929, construction began on U.S. Highway 43 to connect Mobile, Alabama, and Columbia, Tennessee, using convict laborers, and a convict work camp was built on the property of Dr. G. W. Mixon. The new highway brought more traffic and increased commerce to Hackleburg, giving birth to new businesses like this service station.

BLUE BELL AT HACKLEBURG. In the early days, wooden planks covered small ditches or wet areas on the trail from the Blue Bell shirt factory to the buffet lunch at the City Café, the only restaurant in town. A time clock was used to record when each employee entered and exited the building, and at lunchtime, this was a busy walk as employees rushed to get their lunch and be back at work on time.

SHOTTSVILLE COMMUNITY. Pictured are, from left to right, (first row) William Thorton Shotts, John Jerome Shotts, Marcus LaFayette Shotts, and Elliott McCindry Shotts; (second row) John McCarty Shotts, Tilmon LaFayette Shotts, Ambrose Calhoun Shotts, and Ulysesse McDuffy Shotts. The father of the men in the first row, John Shotts, married Frances Stone and settled in Marion County on a homestead in Stonetown. They lived there until 1862. After the battle at Shiloh, Mississippi, and the deaths of two relatives, John moved his large family to Tennessee. John's brother Lovid McCindry Shotts, the father of the men in the second row, moved to the Stonetown community in Marion County. He operated a general store, gristmill, sawmill, cotton gin, and post office. The name of the community was later changed to Shottsville because many members of the Shotts family lived there.

OLD SOUTH SOLDIERS REUNION. A reunion of the Old South Soldiers Union was held in Winfield, most likely in 1899. In attendance from left to right are (first row) John Kelley, Wash Musgrove, unidentified, Ruby Shirey, two unidentified, ? Braswell, unidentified, N. A. Musgrove, Numan Williams, two unidentified, S. W. Moss, Jim Pollard, unidentified, Hezy Cadwell, and unidentified; (second row) Bill Haney, five unidentified, John Wheller, unidentified, Tom Smith, unidentified, Jack Mazingo, John Malot, three unidentified, Matt Trasia, Dr. Sea, Ben Henderson, unidentified, and W. J. Trull.

WINFIELD MAIN STREET. In this July 10, 1926, photograph, the post office is in the upper right corner. The banner across the street reads, "Prayer Meeting at Church of Christ." The Winfield Church of Christ had its beginnings in the late 1880s and early 1890s. Early services of the church were sometimes held in the school building, which was located at that time on the south side of town. In 1895, Elisha Vickery donated the property where the first Church of Christ building stood.

ALABAMA CONCERT IN WINFIELD. A local man had his picture made with traveling entertainers who performed in Winfield. To the right of the band members is little Thurman Dixon Taylor with his father, Wesley Sheld Taylor.

SATURDAY MORNING IN WINFIELD. This photograph was made on Main Street in Winfield about 1900. The farmers pictured above came to town that Saturday for a big sale at Robertson and Harris Mercantile Store (center).

WINFIELD, 1910. Many citizens agree that Winfield was first called Needmore. However, the year the citizens established the first post office and presented the name Needmore to the United States Postal Service, referred to at the time as the Post Office Department, there was already a Needmore, Alabama. Officials then submitted three names to William A. Musgrove for the final decision. It has been said that Musgrove decided upon Winfield, Alabama, because he admired Gen. Winfield Scott so much.

MUSGROVE HOTEL. Nathan Musgrove and his wife, Harriet, first cooked and served meals to railroad workers from their log cabin. They later built the first boardinghouse for the workers of the railroad, then known as the Kansas City, Memphis, and Birmingham Railroad and now as the Frisco Railroad. This first boardinghouse grew into a career of hotel ownership and management for Harriett and Nathan Musgrove, who established the first hotel in Winfield. They operated a hotel for 43 years.

PP Chevrolet Company. Perry and Pate Chevrolet Company was a strong force in Winfield in its day. Winfield was known for being home to PP Chevrolet.

Harris Store in Winfield, 1950s. R. W. Harris and Son was a general merchandise store in Winfield. The store is in business today and owned by Boyd Pate. Walking into the store is like going back in time; one can still see the original store fixtures.

HACKLEBURG BRIDGE. Pictured here in 2003 is the Price Bridge near Hackleburg. Iron bridges were used to provide protection, and truss bridges, like the one shown here, became a common type of bridge built from the 1870s through the 1930s.

BLACK'S GROCERY STORE, 1945. Ralph and Guy Black owned Black's Grocery Store in Guin, opening the store after Ralph returned home from World War II. The Black family lived in the Blowhorn community in Lamar County before moving to Guin.

BRILLIANT COAL COMPANY. The Aldridge brothers opened a coal mine in Brilliant and operated it for some years as the Aldridge Mining Company. They later sold the mine to some people from Birmingham who changed the name to the Brilliant Coal Company. This name was chosen because of the glossy appearance of the coal, which when analyzed, contained only two percent ash, one percent sulphur, and no clinker. Clinker is the coagulated slag or metal impurities that melt from coal as it becomes coke when processed.

BRILLIANT COAL MINING SEAM. This seal of coal and the Montevallo seam located lower in the state were the best domestic seams in the United States, except for several small seams (6 to 8 inches) of candle coal in the states of Kentucky and Colorado, which were too small to mine profitably.

COAL MINER. Zack Rawls is pictured at the mine in 1940. The Montevallo seam has been exhausted for several years, leaving this seam, now known as the Black Creek seam, standing alone as the best domestic coal available.

BRILLIANT COAL OFFICE. In this picture, an employee sits in the front office. When Davis Roberts established the Brilliant Coal Company, he built this structure, which served as his office for some 50 years, across from the railroad and commissary. The building had a porch down one side and in front as well. It also served as the office of bookkeeper Lester McCam and timekeeper Roy Franks. Roberts's private office was located in one of the back rooms.

BRILLIANT STORE. The store would open about 5:30 a.m. on weekdays to accommodate miners who would stop in to fill their lunch buckets and purchase supplies. The miners would then wait on the front porch for their respective rides to certain mining jobs. The store carried items sold for home use such as coal heater, fireplace grates, stovepipe, and coal scuttles. Mining companies also bought supplies like pumps, pipe nails, and electrical wire.

COMPANY DOCTOR'S OFFICE. The coal company furnished a doctor for the miners. In this photograph, the doctor's office and commissary are visible.

BRILLIANT WOODMAN OF THE WORLD, 1911. Joseph Cullen Root founded the Woodman of the World national organization in Omaha, Nebraska, on June 6, 1890. He wanted to have an organization that would clear away problems of financial security for its members. The only person identified in this photograph is Elbert W. Doss (third row, fourth from left).

LOG YARD IN GUIN. Kenny Lumber Company began in Guin soon after the end of World War I, providing jobs for many people. The company later became known as Brown Lumber Company and was sold to Elias Guin on July 20, 1940. In 1946, the company was purchased by Auburn Dennis.

WRIGHT'S STORE IN GUIN. Pictured here from left to right are H. S. Wright, Pet Allman, unidentified, Addie Mae Mills, and Judge Mack Pearce. The Wrights were early settlers of Marion County.

FORD'S MILL. Ford's Mill was established around 1906 when William Basel Ford built a rock dam on Ragsdale Creek. This rock dam was replaced in 1949. Ford's Mill served Hamilton and the surrounding areas for many years. It closed in the late 1960s or early 1970s. Ford was married to Icy Hamilton.

Mae Wiginton Williams. Teaching school in Brilliant in the early 1930s was a challenging job, but Mae Wiginton Williams endured the hardships, always putting the children's education first. She is the granddaughter of Thomas Wesley Wiginton, who served as commissioner of Marion County in the early 1900s, and the sister of Willie Wiginton Fikes.

Sim Williams, Mail Carrier for Guin Route. The mail was carried by horse and buggy and involved some very severe hardships due to the extremely cold weather and bad roads.

CAUDLE MILL, 1880s. Steve Caudle owned and operated the first sawmill in Guin. Names on the photograph are listed as (1) John Morrow, (2) William Pope, (3) Robert Hope Caudle, (4) Old Silas, (5) Anthey Metcalf, (6) Eddie Caudle (Miles's son), (7) Dave Morrow, (8) Tom Caudle, (9) Miles Caudle, (10) George Crews, and (11) Eddie Crews. Stephen Caudle Jr. also owned a gristmill, cotton gin, and blacksmith shop near Guin, Alabama. Guns were made in the blacksmith shop.

LON WRIGHT, MAIL CARRIER. Two of the early Caudle and early Guin postmasters were Stephen Caudle, appointed postmaster on April 24, 1883, and John L. White, appointed June 6, 1888. Other postmasters included Thomas T. Kirk, Merideth T. Akers, James C. Tidwell, Andrew W. Anthony, John W. Holloway, Lemuel B. McWhirter, Rufus S. Shirey, Mary J. Anthony, Julius N. A. Hulsey, T. Jesse Holloway, and James C. Mattox.

34

WINFIELD MAIL CARRIER. James Andrew Patterson started in the Rural Free Delivery business in 1905 at the Glen Allen Post Office. He was later transferred to the Winfield Post Office. He was in the mail business for 43 years.

GUIN POST OFFICE, 1912. Pictured from left to right are Sim Williams, mail carrier; L. B. McWhirter, postmaster; and Lon Wright, mail carrier. McWhirter was appointed Guin postmaster on September 27, 1907.

MURRAY COBB HOLLIS, M.D. Born in Lamar County, Alabama, Dr. Murray Cobb Hollis started out practicing in a horse and buggy. He practiced medicine from 1908 until 1963. The Alabama Medical Association honored the doctor for his 50 years of service to the medical profession in 1958. He died on August 21, 1965, and is buried in the Winfield City Cemetery.

LLOYD CAUDLE. Pictured around 1916 are, from left to right, Alma Pollard, Lloyd Caudle, Vernalee Pollard, and Wallace Wates. Lloyd Caudle moved to Guin in 1914 to send his three daughters—Lillie, Millie, and Savannah—to school. He was barn boss for the Brown Lumber Company, where he fed and took care of 150 horses and mules used to haul logs to the mill and lumber to the markets. He was also mayor of Guin for two terms.

WHITE'S STORE. In 1877, William R. White formed a partnership with Capt. A. J. Hamilton to open a general store in a log cabin in a settlement known as Toll Gate, Alabama. White hauled the first goods and merchandise in a wagon with a team of mules from Columbus, Mississippi, a distance of 80 miles.

HAWKS ARNOLD STORE C. 1912. In the photograph are, from left to right, John Henry Rudicell, two unidentified, Hawks Arnold, and unidentified. Some farmers who came to town on business brought their own food, but most of them ate canned goods at stores. Foods such as sardines, salmon, tomatoes, peaches, and Vienna sausages were served in dishes, and crackers and pepper sauce were always provided. A good meal in the store cost about 30¢. Credit was available in most stores, especially to farmers who paid their bills after harvest.

JESS ARNOLD STORE. In 1907, the town of Hamilton had approximately 400 people living in 67 houses. The town also had nine stores, including the Jess Arnold Store pictured above; two hotels; two churches, Methodist and Baptist; two schools; two printing offices, one of which published a weekly newspaper; two law offices; one barbershop; one blacksmith shop; a post office; courthouse; jail; ball field; and graveyard. However, there were no restaurants.

LISTER HILL HOSPITAL. This photograph was taken shortly after the construction of the hospital in Hamilton in the early 1950s. Lister Hill was chairman of the Senate Labor and Public Welfare Committee, which handled important legislation on veterans's education, health, hospitals, libraries, and labor-management relations. He was also a ranking member of the Senate Appropriations Committee and a member of the Senate Democratic Policy Committee.

BEXAR COTTON GIN. It is not known when the Bexar cotton gin began, but it was still ginning in 1924. In 1934, Gaines Robinson sold it to Oscar Lochridge and Goston Spearman, both from Tremont, Mississippi. Spearman later sold his part due to health. The gin then belonged to Oscar Lochridge, his sons Wendell and Kenneth Lochridge, and son-in-law Max Grady.

COTTONSEED. Cotton was brought to the Bexar gin on wagons and trucks. The cotton, with seed, was weighed on scales, and suction was used to get it into the gin. This picture shows the gin head, where saws separated the seed and cotton. The seed was blown in the seed house, and the lent went upstairs to a press to be made into a bale held together with four ties. Some people saved the seed; some swapped it for cottonseed meal and hulls for cow feed, both by-products of the ginning process done at Ogden's gin in Sulligent, Alabama.

LYMAN RAY'S FEED AND SEED STORE. Pictured in the feed and seed store are James Ray, Greal Lindsey, and Doc Palmer. Lyman Ray farmed and did some construction work. He owned the feed and seed store in Hamilton for several years and was part owner of the Hamilton Gin Company and Hamilton Grain and Elevator. Ray's two sons, Charles Woodie and Johnny, both live in Hamilton today and are active in the community.

SNOW IN HACKLEBURG. In this photograph, Hackleburg's streets are covered with snow. In the early days of Hackleburg, snow fell most winters, but in recent years, weather patterns have changed and not very much snow falls.

WINFIELD GAS STATION. Years ago, filling stations usually sold gasoline, oil, and service. If one stopped to put gas in the car, the oil and the air in the tires would be checked and the windshield would be washed.

42

OLD HAMILTON MILL. Capt. A. J. Hamilton built this mill in the late 1800s on Williams Creek. It burned, and another mill was constructed. When the Marion County Courthouse was moved from Pikeville to Toll Gate, the name of the town was changed from Toll Gate to Hamilton to honor Captain Hamilton. Captain Hamilton organized Company 7, 5th Mississippi Cavalry and was elected captain in the War between the States.

SECOND HAMILTON MILL. After his first mill burned, Captain Hamilton built this mill for grinding only corn. Captain Hamilton married Mary L. Terrell, daughter of John Dabney Terrell Jr. Hamilton was a planter, and in 1893, owned 8,000 acres of land.

OLD WILLIAMS CREEK BRIDGE. A. J. Hamilton's mill was near this bridge. Captain Hamilton was a Democrat, was elected sheriff for one term, and represented Marion County in the state legislature in the sessions of 1869, 1874, and 1875. Joel Palmer, a local historian, tells tales of growing up on Williams Creek. One story goes, "Somebody said, 'Poor mules, they have to work so hard for so little.' My dad said, 'The mule gets as much, if not more, out of the corn crop than we do. He eats about 20 ears of corn a day, and not counting the hay, in a year's time that will get about half of the corn crop I guess.'" This bridge is still standing today.

ROLLINS COTTON GIN. The Rollins family operated the cotton gin in Hamilton, pictured above, for several years. The family prospered, but the day of the gin is gone.

CARNATION MILK TRUCK. Rex Williford drove the milk truck for the Carnation Milk Company in the early 1950s. Williford collected milk cans from local milk producers in Marion County and hauled the milk to Tupelo, Mississippi, to be processed by Carnation Milk.

COTTON WAGON. The photograph was taken at Bill Perry's cotton warehouse located behind PP Chevrolet in Winfield. Identified are John Haney, far left; Bill Perry, front edge of wagon; and Boyd Ashton, holding reins to the mules.

WINFIELD GIN. The gin in this photograph was located south of the railroad behind Vickery Trading Post. In 1892, there were two gins in Winfield: Webster and Jones Gin and Farmer's Alliance and Cotton Yard.

A. J. Hamilton House. This photograph appears to have been taken outside the A. J. Hamilton house; all the men are probably county and town officials. In 1882, an election was held in Marion County to select a new courthouse location. Toll Gate won the election, a new courthouse was erected, and the court, court officials, and records were moved. The Toll Gate name was changed in honor of Capt. A. J. Hamilton, who donated 40 acres of his plantation to be sold in lots to help cover the cost of building the courthouse. The name of the Toll Gate Post Office was changed to Hamilton Post Office on November 17, 1882.

PEPSI TRUCK. Pepsi-Cola Dr. Pepper Bottling Company, Inc., has been part of the Winfield community for a long time. This company is a large supporter of Winfield's annual Mule Day, held the fourth Saturday in September each year. Celebrating its 25th anniversary in 2008, Mule Day has grown into a major event not only for the city of Winfield but also for the state of Alabama, drawing crowds of over 25,000 each year.

MUSGROVE STORE. Willie Bruce Musgrove came to Winfield in the late 1800s and went into the general merchant business. He is pictured here in July 1927 in his general store, which was located across the alley from the original Citizens Bank of Winfield. Musgrove retired in 1945.

WINFIELD STORE. Pictured in the Sizemore and Ward General Store in Winfield are Raymond Sizemore (left) and Cliff Vernon.

M. V. WHITE GROCERY. In the photograph are, from left to right, E. E. Ivie, M. V. White, Hook Wallace, Jar Mills, and Dewey Harris. This store was located adjacent to the railroad on U.S. Highway 43 South.

GET YOUR *SATURDAY EVENING POST*. Bert Doss, son of photographer J. H. Doss, is shown around 1913 in his best peddling pose. *The Saturday Evening Post* published current event articles, editorials, human-interest pieces, humor, illustrations, a letter column, poetry (including work written by readers), cartoons, and stories.

MODEL T, 1913. Pictured from left to right are two unidentified persons, R. R. Wright, Gladys Wright, and Raymond Wright about 1915. Probate judge George W. Pearce died in office in March 1947, and R. R. Wright was appointed to serve as probate judge of Marion County until the election. Frank Pearce was elected in 1948.

MODEL A ERA. Pictured here is the Wright Motor Company around 1932. In the early days, when Wright sold a car, he had to teach the buyer how to drive it. The Ford Motor Company brought the first farm tractor in the county to Wright Motor Company. People from all over the area came to see the tractor demonstrated. The consensus of opinion was that it would never work. The 20 millionth Ford was also brought to Guin in a caravan. Both schools came to town to see the display. Ford brought professional photographers, who took pictures of the car and the schoolchildren.

WRIGHT MOTOR COMPANY. Upon graduation from Sam Houston Teachers College in Huntsville, Texas, R. R. Wright came to Guin in 1905 as cashier of the Bank of Guin, the first bank in Marion County. Soon afterwards, the bank also started service in the Hamilton area, and the name was changed to Marion County Banking Company. Wright served as cashier until 1913, at which time he opened a Ford agency known as the Wright Motor Company in Guin. He sold the first Model T to mail carrier Ivy Thompson, who delivered on the Guin star mail route, which ran from Guin, Alabama, to Hamilton, Alabama. Wright also purchased his first car at this time. According to R. R. Wright, the first car in Guin was owned by Gus Hallmark, who purchased his car in Birmingham one month before Wright opened his business. Wright filled the area with Model T cars, selling 615 in a three-year period.

Two

PEOPLE

JUDGE D. TERRELL JR. The son of John Dabney Terrell Sr. served as probate judge in Marion County for 45 years. John was a very learned and astute person who grew up with the politics that surrounded his father. Judge Terrell Jr. loved money and became a wealthy man. When times were hard for the local citizens, he used his wealth as the only banker around to help his needy neighbors through an economic depression.

DR. BUSBY AND DR. MASON. S. S. Busby, M.D., and Robert Mason, M.D., are pictured at the hospital in Hamilton. Two early physicians in Marion County were Dr. John Mangrum, who came from the Newberry district in South Carolina, and Dr. M. H. Key, who moved from Georgia in 1854.

DR. STEPHEN SAMPSON BUSBY. Busby graduated from Birmingham Medical College in 1908 and began a practice in Marion County in 1927. Known as "Samp" or "Doc," he practiced medicine from the horse-and-buggy days, through Model T days, and on to the time of the modern car. He lived to see the first man on the moon.

Mixon Store in Hamilton. Pictured from left to right are Carl Ford, Bankhead Mixon, and J. B. Hodges. Bankhead Mixon was the son of George Brown Mixon, who owned a general merchandise store in Hamilton. Descendants continued to operate the store under the Mixon name until 1994.

Mixon Family. Pictured from left to right are (first row) George Brown Mixon and Sarah Jane Sanderson Mixon; (second row) Wesley Mixon, James Henry Mixon, and John Bankhead Mixon. George Wesley Mixon graduated from West Alabama Agricultural School in Hamilton in 1900. He then attended the University of Alabama Medical College in Mobile, Alabama, graduating from medical school in 1904 and opening a practice in Hackleburg, Alabama. In addition to his medical practice, Dr. Mixon was one of five aldermen elected after Hackleburg was incorporated on August 23, 1909.

WILLIE WIGINTON AND LOUIS ELAINE FIKES MARRY. This photograph was taken on April 22, 1951, the Fikes's wedding day. Many Marion County residents knew Willie from her work with the USDA Farmers Home Administration, from which she is now retired. Louis Elaine Fikes obtained a Chevrolet dealership in November 1978, serving the public in and around Hamilton for almost 30 years before his death. Their sons, Jeffrey and John Fikes, operate the business now.

WILLIAM R. WHITE IN LATER YEARS. White was appointed the first postmaster of Toll Gate when the post office was established on March 7, 1878. When the name of the Toll Gate office was changed to Hamilton on November 17, 1882, he was reappointed postmaster and served until May 25, 1889.

WHITE ROCK. On Sunday afternoons in good weather, couples would meet at a certain location and take walks or buggy rides. One of the favorite spots was about 1 mile north of Hamilton, just off U.S. Highway 43, at White Rock, appropriately named as it consists of a series of white rock bluffs that stretch out along the Buttahatchee River. It contains a solid sandstone rock bluff about 200-feet-high that runs about 1 mile along the riverbank. The location is noted for having been a prison camp during the Civil War.

WHITE ROCK CAMP. White Rock is also the site where the notorious Ham Carpenter was put to death. Carpenter, a Southerner, became a feared terrorist during the Civil War, renowned for burning people out of their homes, destroying their life-supporting crops, and, worst of all, killing many innocent people. He was finally captured and taken to White Rock, where he was put to death.

LES PEARCE AND STELLA BAIRD. White Rock had perfect scenery for picture taking. Usually when Sunday afternoon strollers were enjoying the site, a photographer would be nearby. He would take photographs of individuals, couples, or entire groups, and in a few days, he would try to sell the pictures to them.

YOUNG MEN. Roy Alexander was the son of George Alexander, who came from South Lamar County and lived north of Guin on Beaver Creek in the Lolley community. George Alexander sold his farm to Henry Guin and moved to Guin in 1913 or 1914. He was in the mercantile business for many years. Pictured are, from left to right, unidentified, Roy Alexander, and Hewitt Pearce.

PHOTOGRAPH OF YOUNG MEN. In another photograph, the young men from above are seen here without their coats. From left to right are unidentified, Roy Alexander, and Hewitt Pearce.

CHILDREN AND GOAT. The precious children in this photograph are unidentified, but this is a nice ride for baby.

COUPE IN 1930. In this photograph is Johnny and Estelle Parks's coupe with little Mary C. Reese sitting on the runner. In 1880, there were 27 persons living in Marion County with the last name Reese. By 1900, there were only four persons with the Reese name living in Marion County.

BABY BUGGY. Baby Mary Calhon Reese is pictured here on January 4, 1928. She was the daughter of Calhon and Mary E. Peeler Littleton Reese.

ELI GUIN FAMILY. In the photograph from left to right are Viola, Eli, Joel, Mary E., and Flex. The family was very influential during the establishment of Guin.

PEARCE HOTEL. Pictured from left to right are (first row) three unidentified, Lillian Ling Sizemore, Lula Ling Nettles, and four unidentified; (second row) three unidentified, Harkins Guin, and eight unidentified; (third row) three unidentified, Red Pope, Stella Guin, and ten unidentified; (fourth row) two unidentified, Pearl Stanford Sizemore, and Viola Guin. The exact location of Guin's Pearce Hotel is not known at this time.

SHELTON FAMILY. Pictured is Dr. W. H. Shelton with his children and a family friend. From left to right are Edna Shelton, Dr. Sam Shelton, Dr. W. H. Shelton, Carey Walker, and Craig Shelton. Dr. W. H. Shelton married Kate Frazier in 1889 in Hamilton. They moved to Guin with Kate's parents in 1895. Shelton and his father-in-law, Madison M. Frazier, were in general merchandise. After the loss of his first son, W. H. Shelton desired more than ever to become a doctor. He graduated from the University of Tennessee School of Medicine in 1901 and returned to Guin, serving for many years as a country doctor. In the early years, he would walk at night, even in the winter, to visit sick patients he could not reach by buggy.

WHITE ANTHONY FAMILY. (Andrew) White Anthony married Louzette Jones in 1883. He farmed near Guin until 1901, when he received a post office appointment under Teddy Roosevelt and moved to town. In 1901, he took over postmaster duties at the Guin Post Office. Mary Jane Anthony, the oldest of White and Louzette Anthony's seven children, was his assistant. She was 16 years old at the time. Anthony succeeded a Mr. Tidwell, who moved to Texas. Tidwell had also employed his own daughter, Clara Tidwell, as his assistant. Anthony served only one four-year term in the post office before John Holloway accepted the position.

ROY ALEXANDER. In the 1910 census of Marion County, there were seven persons listed by the name Alexander; by 1920, there were 30. In 1910, Roy and his family were living in Pikeville beat, and in 1920, they were in Guin beat.

SHIREY CHILDREN. In the photograph are the children of Vada and Willie Baird Shirey. From left to right are Annie Lou, Clark, and Mary. Willie Shirey was Marion County's postmistress. The post office was located near where Marion County Banking now operates.

DR. H. H. SIZEMORE AND LILLIAN LING MARRY. This couple married on June 16, 1914. Dr. Sizemore was the son of Thomas Henry and Eugenia Ellen "Mollie" Middleton Sizemore. Mollie raised nine children, managed a home on a 500-acre farm, and helped her husband in the post office, which was in their house at first. She took care of her children and saw that their home was the center of their social life. In 1896, L. Y. Powers was the first dentist in town, followed by Dr. H. H. Sizemore, Dr. Bill White, and Dr. Mark Hall.

JOHN AND MARY CORBETT. The Corbetts moved to Guin in 1916. Their son Grady boarded in Guin and attended Marion County High School two years before his parents moved to the area. Unfortunately, he died before he finished school. In the 1920 Marion County census, there were 11 persons by the name Corbett. The name "Corbett" was taken from Shropshire, England, to Scotland in the 12th century, to northern Ireland in the 17th century, and later brought to North America.

MEN AT COURTHOUSE. These young men are all unidentified except for Roy Alexander (first row, center) and Hewett Pearce (first row, right).

VADA SHIREY. After the deaths of their parents, Vada Shirey and siblings came to Guin to live with their grandparents, John and Elimira Hughes, in the fall of 1901. Vada worked for L. Pearce in the merchandise business and later in the post office. He married Willie Baird, the daughter of Steve Baird.

PEARCE HOTEL. Pictured are, from left to right, (first row) three unidentified, Lula Ling Nettles, Viola Guin, Ruth Shaw, and four unidentified; (second row) three unidentified, Lillian Ling Sizemore, four unidentified, Pearl Stanford Sizemore, two unidentified, Callie Stanford, and unidentified; (third row) unidentified, Stella Guin, unidentified, Pauline Springfield, and Willie Baird Shirey.

RUFUS BAIRD. Baird was Marion County sheriff for a number of years. Sheriff Baird's wife, Sarah, was a faithful member of the Baptist church in Guin. While he was sheriff, she would read the Bible to the people he locked up. Following his terms as sheriff, Rufus and his brother Stephen owned and operated Baird Mercantile store in Guin.

STEPHEN BAIRD HOUSE. Baird was born September 1857 in Chickasaw County, Mississippi, and in 1880, he married Emily Bexley Clark in Marion County, Alabama. After his wife's death, he moved to Henryetta, Oklahoma. He died there in 1942 and was brought back to be buried in the Guin City Cemetery.

ALLMAN KIDS. Pictured are, from left to right, Ervin Allman, Pettus Allman, and Pearce Allman. In 1905, their father, John Allman, was said to be the ramrod in the Bank of Guin organization, which later became the Marion County Banking Company. He remained an official of this bank until his death in 1939.

ASTON FAMILY. Among the family members pictured are, in no particular order, Sally ?, Hettie Aston Guin, C. C. Guin, Dan Kleckley, Newman Aston, Margret Smith, Jessie Guin Searcy, Lucy Guin Pratt, R. B. Smith, Lucy Aston Smith, Charlie Aston, Melissa Aston, Molly Aston, Oak Aston, Ettie Aston May, Della Aston Stuart, Fenton Aston, Mamie Aston Caddell, Jim Caddell, and Maggie Kleckley.

ELI GUIN FAMILY. Eli Guin married Emmaline Hilburn in the 1890s. The Hilburns lived near the present site of the elementary school, and Eli Guin had a home near the school as well. The Guin children were Joel Wood, Arvilla, Wilma, Viola, Eunice, Harkins, Stella, and Icy Banks. Joel Wood was the first graduate from Marion County High School in 1912; Viola had a millinery shop. Members of the Eli Guin family are among the people pictured above, in no particular order.

FORBUS COLLINS HOUSE. J. Forbus Collins came to Guin in early 1880. He was a carpenter and built the third house in Guin on 30 acres of land he bought for $200. He was married to Frances Cash, and they had three children—two that died as infants and Will A. Collins. Forbus Collins was elected mayor in 1890, the second mayor after incorporation. The Collins family later moved to Lamar County in the late 1890s. Frances Cash Collins was the first resident buried in the city cemetery.

JIM RILEY AND HUEL MIXON. Jim Riley moved his family to Marion County in a covered wagon in 1879. They settled in the Philadelphia community, and he worked at the courthouse in Pikeville. In 1881, when the county seat moved from Pikeville to Hamilton, he laid out the streets in Hamilton and Guin. He built a home near the Buttahatchee River on the Lamar County line. His wife died, and when he moved to Guin, he had her body moved to the Guin City Cemetery.

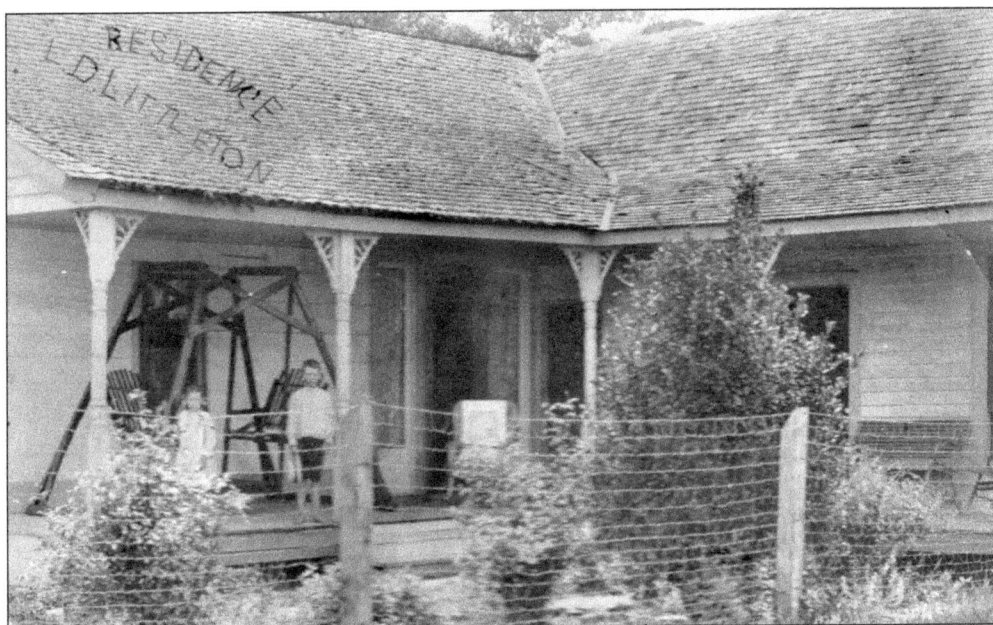

LITTLETON HOUSE. Mary E. Reese's smile attracted the attention of L. D. Littleton, a Guin banker and merchant. She married him in 1916, at which time she joined Guin Methodist Church to worship with the Littleton family. Upon Littleton's death in January 1920, she was left with two small children, three mercantile stores, director's duties at the Marion County Banking Company, hundreds of acres of farmland, and the responsibility of supporting 40 farm families until harvest and settlement time.

MARY E. LITTLETON, C. 1921. Mary E. Littleton was born Marietta Peeler on March 17, 1886. Following business school, she worked for her brother using her typing and bookkeeping skills until she got employment at Pearce's Mill. At that time, social pressures were great against a girl having any gainful employment except teaching. Mary changed her given name to two words in order to have a middle initial for business usage. She bought a 200-acre farm, mules, a wagon, and farm machinery during her seven-year employment. She later married L. D. Littleton.

OAK ASTON FAMILY. Pictured are, from left to right, (first row) Oak, Lucy, Charlie, Molly with Fenton on her lap, Della, and Sally Aston; (second row) Eddy, Hettie, Newman, Maggie, and Mamie Aston.

PAUL CAUDLE. This 1917 photograph shows Paul Caudle and an unidentified woman. Caudle served as mayor of Guin from 1922 to 1923. The Caudles operated a mill in 1886 when the railroad was being built through Guin. They also had a blacksmith shop. This shop was used in making and repairing implements for farming, repairing buggies and wagons, and making guns and horse and mule shoes.

WILLIE BAIRD SHIREY. Willie Baird, daughter of Steve Baird, married Vada Shirey of Guin. They moved to Henryetta, Oklahoma, in 1927. They had several children.

HAMILTON CITY COUNCIL, 1953. Pictured here from left to right are Frances Loden, Gene Lindsey, Clint Green, Mayor James Lunsford, Jack Lindsey, and Odie Cooper at a city council meeting. The city of Hamilton is governed by a mayor and five council members elected by voters to serve four-year terms.

HAMILTON CITY COUNCIL. Seen here from left to right are (seated) Gene Lindsey, Odie Cooper, Mayor James Lunsford, Frances Loden, Jack Lindsey, and Clint Green; (standing) Fred Stidham, Ellis Gunnin, and Junior Tyra.

HAMILTON POLICEMEN, 1950S.
Pictured here are Ellis Gunnin
(left) and Junior Tyra.

JAMES PERRY SANDERSON.
Sanderson's friends called him
"Jim." He is listed in the 1900
Marion County Census with
his wife and three sons in the
Barnesville community. He
died on January 24, 1945.

JOHN LEONARD WEEKS (1837–1926).
Weeks married Susan Thomas Vickery. He fought in the Civil War, first with the 16th Alabama Infantry. His first major battle was at Mill Springs (Fishing Creek), Kentucky. He also fought in the battle of Shiloh, and during the retreat into Mississippi, he left his unit. Next he fought with the First Mississippi Cavalry. He was wounded and captured in a skirmish in Mississippi and held as a prisoner of war at Alton Prison in Alton, Illinois, where he was treated for smallpox.

MILLIGAN WEEKS. Jackson Milligan Weeks came to Guin in March 1917 from Beaverton, Alabama, after selling a cotton gin, a water-run gristmill, and a hotel there. He came to Guin so that his children could attend high school, the only one close by. Known as Milligan, he operated a gristmill at the corner of Eleventh Avenue and Tenth Street. He later bought a sawmill, gristmill, and cotton gin located on the Old Mill Pond.

MARION COUNTY COURTHOUSE IN BACKGROUND. Pearl Shackelford Lawhon (1889–1972), wife of E. C. Lawhon Sr., is believed to be the person on the horse at left.

SUNDAY AFTERNOON. Here is another photograph of a group at White Rock out for some fresh air and possibly "courting." The photographer was always nearby to capture the moment.

CEREMONY AT COURTHOUSE. This appears to be a ceremony outside the courthouse in Hamilton. The men look to be in Masonic dress.

LEE CRUMP, U.S. MARSHAL. Crump had homes in both Lamar and Marion Counties. He was a Deputy U.S. Marshall and one of the pioneers of law enforcement in the area, having been a deputy sheriff for a number of years. Lee Crump was respected and known throughout the state. Crump moved his family from the Henson Springs community in Lamar County to Guin in 1926 because the high school in Guin was thought to provide a better education.

STIDHAM FAMILY. Winston Dilmus Stidham bought about 800 acres of Native American land. The old log house shown above was built on some of this land. The man pictured is Stidham's youngest child, Dilmus LaFayettte Stidham, with his wife, Ellen Lindsey Stidham, and their grandson J. D. Stidham.

DILMUS LAFAYETTTE STIDHAM. Most Stidham immigrants to the United States came from Liverpool, England, and Queenstown, Ireland. Civil War records reveal that 77 Stidham men pledged allegiance to the Confederacy, and 30 Stidham men pledged allegiance to the Union.

BROTHER AND SISTER. In the photograph are Bertie Louise Aston, who married Fred Musgrove, and her brother Emmit Rabie Aston. They are the children of Henry Walter Aston and Dora W. McDonald.

WIGINTON FAMILY CELEBRATES. In this photograph, family and friends of Thomas Wesley Wiginton have gathered together to celebrate his 77th birthday. He served as a Marion County commissioner c. 1900 and was in office when the decision was made to build the stone courthouse.

WILLIAM RANDOLPH WHITE AND SON. During the 1870s, White attended the Vernon District School in Vernon, Alabama, and Southern University in Greensboro, Alabama. He taught at several Marion County schools. As a young man, White had clerked for Capt. A. J. Hamilton at his store in Pikeville, Alabama, in 1873. He later served for six years as probate judge.

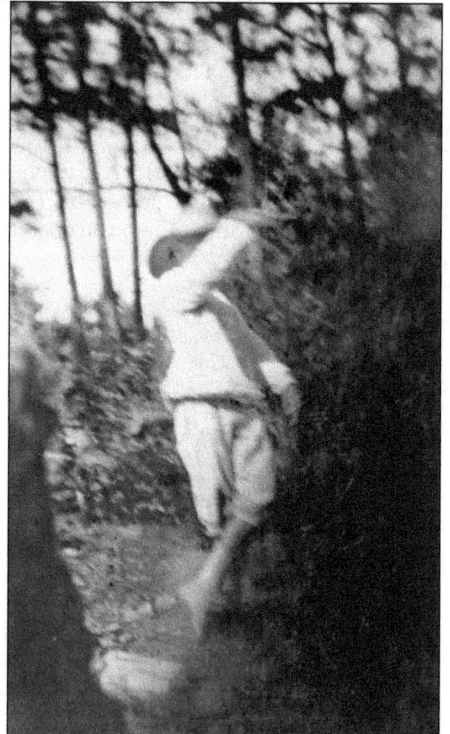

WILLIAM BYRD MCDONALD. "Willie B." McDonald strikes a humorous pose in this photograph. He owned the McDonald hotel in Winfield.

FLOODED RIVER. This photograph was found in the personal collection of Rubye Aston Jefferies. From left to right in the skiff are Alexander White McDonald, unidentified, Walter McDonald, and Boss McDonald. They are the sons of William Byrd McDonald and Mary Ann Bishop. The McDonald family lived in a house that is still occupied in Winfield, Alabama.

WORLD WAR I. Wilburn Aston, son of Henry Walter Aston and Dora W. McDonald, reported for duty in World War I.

WILLIAM CLARK WEBSTER FAMILY. Pictured from left to right are Leona Ollie Webster, William Clark Webster, Pervy Webster, Sarah Dodson Webster, and Rhoda Catherine "Tass" Webster. William Clark Webster (1939–1894), son of Samuel Clark Webster, was a sergeant in the 5th Alabama Cavalry, CSA. He married Sarah Elizabeth Dodson (1842–1929), daughter of Horace D. Dodson and Mary "Polly" South. The Webster home, once located in Winfield, is no longer in existence.

HENRY WALTER ASTON FAMILY, C. 1900. From left to right are Henry Walter Aston, Emmit Rabie Aston on his father's lap, William Wilburn Aston, Andrew Moody Aston, Gracie Mae Aston, and Dora W. McDonald Aston. More children were born later. The family lived in Winfield, Alabama, across the street from the McDonalds. Henry Walter "Walt" Aston (1860–1923) was the son of Andrew Milligan Aston and Manerva Jane Morton. In 1892, Walt married Dora Wilmerth McDonald, daughter of William Byrd McDonald and Mary Ann Bishop.

WILLIAM BYRD MCDONALD (1841–1901). Pictured from left to right are (first row) Dora McDonald Aston with Wilburn Aston sitting on her lap, Andy Aston, and William Byrd McDonald; (second row) William Byrd "Boss" McDonald, Walter McDonald, and Mary Ann Bishop McDonald; (third row) Jim McDonald, George McDonald, and White McDonald. William Byrd, son of Andrew Alexander McDonald and Elizabeth Prechia Howell, married Mary Ann Bishop, daughter of Pinckney Bishop and Charlotte Pope. He served in the 1st Alabama Cavalry. This family lived in Winfield, Alabama.

CADILLAC IN GLEN ALLEN. Brother William Edwin Patterson (1911–1991) and sister Mildred Virginia Patterson (1916–2007) play in a "Cadillac" at their home in Glen Allen. They are the children of James Andrew Patterson and Lena Estelle Musgrove. They lived in the section of Glen Allen that is enumerated in Marion County.

MUSGROVE HOTEL OWNERS. Nathan Musgrove, son of Tilden and Susannah Musgrove, and his wife, Harriet Susannah Smith, owned the Musgrove Hotel in Winfield, Alabama, located close to the railroad station. Harriet, often called Aunt Harriet, was well known for her superior cooking skills at the hotel.

MUSGROVE STORE. Pictured from left to right are Lena Estelle Musgrove Patterson, Fred Musgrove, Ollie Myrtle Musgrove, Esca Lee Musgrove Lancaster, Martha Adeline Webster Musgrove, and William Bruce Musgrove. William Bruce "Willie B." Musgrove, son of William Anderson Musgrove and Mary Frances Amelia Harris, operated a merchandise store for many years in downtown Winfield, directly across the alley from the bank. He built a home a couple of blocks away at the location of the former post office, across the street from the Baptist church.

FIRST CAR IN WINFIELD. Written on the back of this photograph is the following: "First car in Winfield." However, this statement is not verified. Pictured are, from left to right, (front seat) Bertie Louise Aston and Roy Dalton Caddell; (back seat) Albert Belton Caddell, son of Lewis Green Caddell and Ella J. Musgrove, and Grace Mae Aston, sister of Bertie. Monya Havekost is in possession of this photograph.

FOUNDER OF MUSGROVE METHODIST. John Tilden Musgrove (1793–1875) married Susannah Thompson (1801–1882) on January 9, 1820, in Tuscaloosa, Alabama. They were enumerated in the 1830 Marion County Census. She was the daughter of Nathan Thompson (b. 1775) and Elizabeth Weaver (b. 1776). Tilden Musgrove is the founder of Musgrove Chapel United Methodist Church in Winfield, Alabama.

ALBERT JAMES HAMILTON JR. The home of Albert James Hamilton Jr. stands today at 208 Flowers Avenue in Hamilton, Alabama. He was the son of Capt. Albert James Hamilton Sr. and Mary Louise Terrell Hamilton. Albert James Jr. died in 1939 and his wife, Nettie, died in 1961; they are both buried in the Captain A. J. Hamilton Memorial Cemetery.

WILLIAMS CREEK. From left to right are Lonie Hamilton and Clem Sullins, probably out on a Sunday afternoon. Legends are told of incidents happening along Williams Creek such as revivals, moonshine making, and even murder.

PRACTICE, 100 YEARS. Rankin Fite, son of Ernest Fite, joined his father's practice in 1939. The office building at 123 First Avenue SW, commonly referred to as the "White House," was a white, one-story, wood-frame office building, which still exists and is being restored on the northwest corner of the firm's new office location. Rankin Fite's grandfather, Bloomer Rankin Fite, began the practice in the late 1880s. Four of Bloomer's sons became lawyers: Arthur, Fred, Kelly, and Ernest.

MODEL T FORD. This is an unidentified family from Winfield posing with their Model T car. Henry Ford once said of the Model T, "I will build a car for the great multitude. It will be large enough for the family, but small enough for the individual to run and care for. It will be constructed of the best materials, by the best men to be hired, after the simplest designs that modern engineering can devise. But it will be low in price that no man making a good salary will be unable to own one—and enjoy with his family the blessing of hours of pleasure in God's great open spaces."

WINFIELD LIVERY STABLE. Pictured here are Hal Ashton and Joel B. Trimm. The livery stable was located in downtown Winfield about where the Baptist church stands today.

MEN OUTSIDE COURTHOUSE. It was reported in the *Montgomery Advertiser* on June 1, 1913, that the non-jury term of the circuit court had been in session in Hamilton. Charles L. Townes, state examiner of public accounts, examined the book of the Marion County officers then in office and the officers who had formerly served the county. There had been no examination of the books for state or county by a state examiner for six years. The books were found to be in good condition. Several small errors were corrected by the examiner, and in some cases, accounts were charged against the officer, but the full text of the report has not been made public.

FIRST SCHOOL IN GUIN. All are unidentified. In 1888, the first school was constructed on a site near the present-day Tombigbee Electric Cooperative, Inc., building. The school was used for many public meetings, both political and civic, and for an occasional entertaining concert. During the summer months, the building was used as a singing school under the direction of Harris Holcomb.

Three

EDUCATION AND RELIGION

METHODIST CHURCH, BRILLIANT. The church and parsonage were built in the early 1920s by local coal miners. The church serves as the cornerstone of the town as visitors travel Main Street from the south. Its architecture is unlike any other structure in town, with its high-pitched roof and stained-glass windows. The church still holds weekly services.

MARION COUNTY HIGH SCHOOL TEAM. Pictured from left to right are (first row) right end Ben Henson, left guard Babe Henson, right guard Dick Henson, center Rex Wright, right tackle Bankhead Akers, left tackle W. E. Dyer, and right end Orville Lee Wilson; (second row) quarterback Gray Springfield; (third row) Tyler Savage, Prentiss Harrison, Clay Guin, and Billy Springer; (fourth row) coach M. E. Smith and coach Roy Davis.

HACKLEBURG TEAM, 1925. Pictured are, from left to right, (first row) Jeff Feltman, Moody Hudson, Henry Farr, Ernest Kennedy, Alma Miller, Dellous Young, and Chester Foster; (second row) O. C. Ernest, Foy Frederick, James Ernest, Leon Wiginton, Dar Hudson, Valers Gann, ? Fincher, Little Clyde Evans, Clyde Frederick, Clyde (Buck) Evans, and Earl Graham.

GUIN BALL TEAM. Pictured from left to right are (first row) Garvin Pope, Dave Holloway, John Shirey, and Bob Holloway; (second row) Jim Davidson, Emmett Shirey, Hewett Pearce, and Craty Corbett; (third row) Gus Hallmark and three unidentified.

FROG POND SCHOOL, 1926–1927. From left to right are (first row) Beatrice Arthur Ballard, Alma Sullins Carlton, Anna Rae Davis Manscill, Flora Clement Harris, and Bessie Sullins Wright; (second row) teacher Wes Taylor, George Palmer, Veola Avery Williams, Taft Williams, Lillian Palmer Williams, Roger Avery, and Springer Anglin; (third row) Colen Skinner, Travis Williams, Lynon Cox, and Clyde Jackson.

IRDINE SHIREY. Shirey was a schoolteacher in Guin, which was well known for its Marion County High School. Many families moved to Guin in order to give their children an opportunity to have a good education.

SUMMER SINGING SCHOOL IN GUIN. Pictured is a music class taught by Mr. Harris Holcolm. During the summer months, the first school building in Guin was used as a "singing school." Mr. Holcomb taught music to interested pupils and occasionally entertained the public with a musical concert. The school building pictured was used for many public meetings, both political and civic, until Marion County High School opened in 1912.

HACKLEBURG SCHOOL. Early schools usually had only one or two teachers, and the building usually did not have many windows. The very first school building for Hackleburg was a log house where the Congregational Church also met. When the Cedar Tree Methodist Church was erected, the school moved there. A school building for grades one through seven was constructed on the Boyd farm in 1913. This building burned in 1921, and classes were held in various churches until 1923.

HAMILTON ELEMENTARY SCHOOL, 1907. In the fall of 1895, the District Agricultural School and Experiment Station was established in Hamilton, where grades one through twelve were taught. This school continued to teach grades one through twelve until the first state-controlled grammar school was built in 1907. It was a three-room building that was situated across the street from the gym that is now a part of Hamilton High School. The three-room building burned in the summer of 1921. The second elementary school building was completed in 1924. It was constructed on the same spot as the first building and was a very modern brick structure.

HAMILTON FIRST BAPTIST. The original site of First Baptist Church is where Loden Furniture Company is currently located. In the summer of 1896, D. N. Cooper gave a plot of land to the then unestablished First Baptist Church of Hamilton. In October 1896, in the Methodist church, First Baptist Church was organized. A frame building was eventually erected on the lot given by Cooper and served as a place of worship for 32 years.

HAMILTON HIGH SCHOOL, 1948. This photograph was taken outside the second high school building, which was completed in 1917 at a cost of $30,000. It burned in 1959. School was first taught in Hamilton in 1884 in a little plank house at the foot of Mitchell Hill (West Bexar Street) by Jim White. The next year, Dr. Marion H. Key and his daughter Elliott Key taught at the school. There was no public money, and all the scholars were called on to pay tuition fees, which supported the school and paid the teachers. The first high school was organized around 1889 with professor William Findley (son-in-law of Dr. Key) as the principal. He was a graduate of the Florence State Normal School, and Elliott Key was his assistant.

HAMILTON CHURCH OF CHRIST. This church began meeting in 1897. The first Christians here met in homes from 1897 until 1905. At that time, there were only about two or three families that belonged to the Church of Christ living in Hamilton. The original site of the Hamilton Church of Christ is on Second Avenue, southeast, in Hamilton.

HAMILTON METHODIST CHURCH. Sometime prior to 1858, there was a circuit (a regular route traveled usually by a preacher or teacher) known as the Bexar Circuit. This circuit included Pine Springs, Wesley Chapel, Smyrna, Ebenezer, Bexar, Newberg, New Bethel, Old Bethlehem, Pleasant Ridge, and possibly other churches. The first circuit rider was Rev. Ethlebert Norton, in 1858. In 1885, a white, wooden structure was erected across from where the B. W. Rollins building stands today.

GUIN CHURCH OF CHRIST. It appears that the Guin Church of Christ congregation began meeting in 1890, or shortly thereafter. It was in this year that Dr. Jerry Guin donated the land for the Baptist, Methodist, and Church of Christ buildings in Guin. History suggests that the congregation first met in a schoolhouse 1 mile from downtown. Later they met downtown where a white, wooden building was constructed.

HACKLEBURG SCHOOL PICTURE. In 1923, a two-story brick school was built on the corner of Clay and Baker Streets. This became the first Hackleburg High School. Grades one through twelve were taught.

HACKLEBURG'S FIRST FOOTBALL TEAM, 1925. Pictured are, from left to right, (first row) Jeff Feltman, Moody Hudson, Henry Farr, Ernest Kennedy, Alma Miller, Dellous Young, and Chester Foster; (second row) Foy Frederick, James Ernest, Leon Wiginton, Dar Hudson, and Valers Gann; (third row) O. C. Ernest, ? Fincher, Little Clyde Evans, Clyde Frederick, Clyde (Buck) Evans, and Earl Graham.

HACKLEBURG SCHOOL 1925–1926. Pictured from left to right are (first row) Clyde Frederick, Clyde Evans, Moody Hudson, Maggie Frederick, Fitz Isom, Foy Frederick, and Lucian Sullins; (second row) Mary Lou Parks, Vera (Bob) Ray, Lorene Freeman, Minnie Lee Boyd, Myrtle Miller, and Venola Cofield; (third row) Carolyn Cofield, Viela Coons, Mona Mixon, Shelly Spratlin, unidentified, Gurt Hall, and Ethel Wiginton; (fourth row) Jessie Lou Mason, Jim Earnest Green, two unidentified, Auta Nix, and two unidentified; (fifth row) unidentified.

FIRST HACKLEBURG SCHOOL BUILDING, 1923. The first graduating class to have attended school in this building was that of the senior class of 1925, which had eight members. Thomas D. Brooks was superintendent of education for Marion County from 1915 to 1933. Francis Cantrell began teaching at Hackleburg High School in 1924 and retired in 1964.

HACKLEBURG SCHOOL BUILDING (1925–1985). In 1936, an elementary school building was constructed on the east side of Nix Road, and the present school occupies those same grounds. A 1943 tornado damaged the high school building's second floor, but the ground floor was usable. Because of the damage, the high school and elementary exchanged buildings.

CIVIL WAR VETERANS REUNION, 1900, WINFIELD. The veterans pictured here are, from left to right, (first row) Alex Rye, S. W. Moses, Ruben Andrew Jackson Dodson Sr., John Erwin, Wash Musgrove, Henry Musgrove, M. T. Akers, John Wheeler, John Harbin, Luther Gilmore, Jake Nix, ? Rawls, and Love and Newman Williams; (second row) Thad Harris, W. R. Haney, H. K. Caddel, ? Bishop, John Berryhill, Landon Mills, W. R. H. Loden, Monroe Ward, Reubin Shirey, Jake Couch, Tommy Smith, Thorn (Thomas) Beasley, Steave Hodges, Jack Mozingo, Ben Henderson, John Jenkins, and John W. Russell; (third row) Isaac Perry, John Hodges, ? Howe, Seay Marcum, William I. Holcomb, Van Miles, Lawson White, Dave Stanford, Elsih Warren, J. B. McClung, S. E. Wier, Abram Shirey, M. A. Musgrove, Doss Mills, John Maddox, and A. J. Fowler (drum).

HACKLEBURG SCHOOL. In 1952, the elementary school burned, and classes were again held in churches. In 1954, an elementary building was constructed on the west side of Nix Road across the street from the high school. Since 1923, high school principals have been Horace Holland, Oscar Earnest, J. S. Brindley, William "Bill" Hill, Ralph Burleson, Max Newman, Wayne Cobb, Ed Allen, Ward Webster, Emmitt Ray, Max Ray, Dan Hindman, and Jerry Kuykendall.

BYRD SCHOOL, C. 1963. The first Byrd School building (named after William A. Byrd, who gave land in the Byrd community) was destroyed by a tornado on April 4, 1920. The community came together, and the Real, Watson, and Byrd Schools were consolidated in order to receive assistance to help construct a new two-story building. Grades one through nine were taught here.

WEST ALABAMA AGRICULTURAL SCHOOL. Alabama had no county high schools in the early 1900s, but in parts of the state, district schools with standards similar to high school had been operating for years. In 1895, the state legislature divided Alabama into nine districts and established a district agricultural school and experiment station in each district. The Sixth District School was located in Hamilton and was called West Alabama Agricultural School.

MOUNT ZION SCHOOL. J. S. Watson taught at Mount Zion School from 1920 to 1921; his salary was $45 per month. This was his first teaching assignment. Pictured above is the school picture for that year. Classrooms were heated by potbellied stoves, and children brought their lunches to school.

AFRICAN AMERICAN SCHOOL. The earliest school for the black people of Guin was conducted in the Methodist church building. Some of the early teachers were Mary Davis, Etta Thompson, and Micha Terrell Warren. Later the community built its own school, a simple wood-frame building with two rooms and more space for the children. The school burned but was built again. Joseph Northington was one of the early teachers at the newer school.

NEW HOME SCHOOL. Lola Annie Isom Mann taught school at New Home, Wiginton, Shiloh, and Gravel Springs in Marion County. All these schools have closed due to consolidation and the changing of times.

NEWBURG SCHOOL. The Newburg School was located in the northwest corner of the county in the Bull Mountain community.

SHOTTSVILLE BASEBALL TEAM, 1901–1902. Pictured are, from left to right, (first row) Bill Cofield, Velera Shotts, Booker Shotts, Oscar Shotts, and Truelove Shotts; (second row) Dewitt Shotts, Veto Shotts, Pole Stone, Clyde Shotts, John Wes Stone, Artemus Shotts, and Emmons Shotts.

SHOTTSVILLE CHURCH. Built in 1936 by Pastor John Hancock and his congregation, this structure was used as the Methodist church until the 1950s. Truelove Shotts is pictured in the doorway.

UNION HILL SCHOOL, 1938. The Union Hill community is about 2 miles south of Hackleburg. In the early days, the county did not own school buses. Men that had trucks would contract with the Marion County School Board to supply a "bus" for schoolchildren. Usually it was a school truck instead of a school bus. The driver did not go by each person's house to pick him or her up; students met the bus at the nearest bus stop to their house.

GUIN, 1932 SIXTH-GRADE CLASS. The only person identified in the photograph is Rex Black (first row, far right). The first public school building in Guin was built in 1888 on a site on the east side of U.S. Highway 78. Many students came from outside the community and boarded.

WINFIELD'S FIRST PUBLIC SCHOOL. C. P. Welden was principal of the first public school in Winfield. Many of the early schools were taught in churches. Early schools usually ran for two months in the summer after crops were laid and for three months in the winter.

BARN CREEK SINGING SCHOOL, 1921. Pictured are those who attended the Barn Creek Singing School. From left to right are (first row) Roy Fredrick, Joel Mann, Loyd Burleson, Talton Mann, Betty Burleson, Glover Burleson, John Tidwell, Lushion Burleson, Leburn Mann, and Ottis Burleson; (second row) Vennie Mann, Vira Burleson, Eunice Frederick, Travie Mann, Ruby Mann, Eunice Burleson, Ora Frederick, Vira Frederick, Ruby Lee Burleson, Prince Burleson, Vira Burleson, ? Tidwell, Frank Burleson, and Polk Tidwell; (third row) Delia Kennedy, Ellie Burleson, Delia Burleson, Mrs. William Sullins, Sherman Tidwell (teacher), Vaudie Burleson, Dora Loden, Ollie Loden, Brell Burleson, and Ervin Armstrong; (fourth row) Ophelia Kennedy, Virgie Burleson, Della Willcutt, Miss Sullins, Cleo Burleson, Jewel Burleson, Pearl Burleson, Ola Burleson, Clara Burleson, Donnie Wilcutt, and Florence Burleson; (fifth row) Archie Loden, Hester Martin, Filo Mays, Mr. Mitchell, George Loden, and Aaron Bailey.

OLD BUTTAHATCHEE SCHOOL IN THE 1920s. This nearly destroyed image shows, in the second window from right, the face of Clyde Burleson, Vera Burleson Wooldridge's father. Second row, third from right is Vera Burleson Wooldridge. Top row, second from left is L. R. Wooldridge. This school building burned.

GUIN FIRST BAPTIST CHURCH. The original church building, completed in 1890, was west of town on Beaver Creek. This church burned, and a new one was built on a lot given by Dr. Jerry Guin. This new location was on old Sulligent Highway at Fourteenth Street and Eleventh Avenue. Records show that Q. Hosmer was pastor in 1890. In 1922, the Church voted to purchase property in the center of town for a new church building. On June 1, 1924, services were held in this new building, which is pictured above.

Four

FORGOTTEN PLACES
AND FACES

BRUSH CREEK
TRESTLE. In northwest
Marion County was
an outstanding feat
of engineering—the
Brush Creek Trestle.
In a March 31, 1981,
article, *Birmingham
News* correspondent
Marj Harris billed it
as "the tallest railway
trestle east of the
Rockies." The first
mail train rolled slowly
across the trestle at
20 miles per hour in
1907, the year that
Bear Creek petitioned
for incorporation.
Built by the Illinois
Central Railroad, the
trestle was nearly 200
feet high and one-
quarter mile long.

TRAGEDY AT BRUSH CREEK. No record has been found of a train accident on Brush Creek Trestle, but there have been other accidents; one man was killed during construction, and Jake Moody, a painter, fell 185 feet to his death in 1939. Tragedy struck again in 1993 when a Phillips High School freshman fell 175 feet in an accident involving a four-wheeler. It was a miracle that he lived; after coming out of a coma and therapy, he could not speak but could use a communications board. The trestle has been dismantled and removed.

PEARCE'S MILL. James (Jim) P. Pearce, the son of John M. W. Pearce, came to Marion County when he was three years old. He had a valorous military record as a veteran of the Mexican War and won the title of captain through gallantry in the Confederate army in the War between the States. Following the Civil War, Jim Pearce returned to the mill his father had built in the 1840s on the Buttachatchee River and found a ravaged countryside. He gradually rebuilt the farm and turned it into both a mill and a trading center. Pearce became one of the largest landholders in Alabama and gained enough power and influence in local political affairs to represent his county at the State Constitutional Convention in 1901. By the early 1870s, Pearce's operation included the gristmill, a large two-story frame general merchandise establishment with post office, a sawmill, a planer, a wheat flour mill, a cotton gin, and freight service. Pictured above is the Pearce home, which at one time also included a post office and Pearce General Merchandise Store.

WOOD COURTHOUSE. The men in this photograph are thought to be members of a grand jury sometime before 1901. The first Marion County courthouse in Hamilton was destroyed by fire on March 30, 1887. It was suggested a new courthouse be built of brick with a tin roof, but it did not work out that way. Notice of the need was put out in the *Marion Herald*. The plans and specifications were adopted, and bids were taken for building the new wood courthouse. Court was held in the lower room of Frasier's and Gast's store in Hamilton during the time the courthouse was being built. The grand jury was held in the upper room of the jail.

PEARCE'S MILL STORE. The Pearce family are said to have owned the first slaves in this community, from the plantation days up to the time that slaves were freed. For many years, Jim Pearce openly opposed the improvements of county roads, fearing they would destroy his store and freight business. He was right. The mill did begin to decline when the roads were improved. As railroads reached the towns and Hamilton, the county seat, these places became more accessible as trading centers. Store operations ceased by 1930, while the mill continued in service until 1959. Marvin Pearce, the son of Jim Pearce, was born in the small village of Pearce's Mill in 1879, had his early schooling in Marion County, and attended both the University of Alabama and Alabama Polytechnic Institute. After college, Marvin was associated with his father in many businesses until his father's death in 1915.

PIKEVILLE. The village of Pikeville was chosen as the site for Marion Court and was confirmed mid-1821. Pikeville was located on Military Road, 7 to 8 miles south of the Military Ford crossing. The name Pikeville was chosen to honor the slain hero of the War of 1812, Gen. Zebulon Pike. Pikeville was surveyed in 1821 and a courthouse built in 1822, but little growth was seen until 1823–1824. Marion County's first official post office was established at Military Ford in 1821 and moved to Pikeville in 1824. The old courthouse still stands.

PIKEVILLE VILLAGE. Pikeville was located on a narrow and isolated ridge along the Military Road among rather poor lands. It did not attract many settlers or many nearby farming ventures. Pikeville, the county seat for 60 years, had no more than 15 business establishments and 20 to 30 homes in 1860. The primary businesses around Pikeville from the 1820s through the 1880s, other than the county court, were tanyards where leather products such as shoes and saddles were made. Pikeville was also noted for beaver-hat production and several good hotels/taverns and saloons. Pikeville society was ably led by probate judge John Dabney Terrell Jr., who mastered county politics and remained in office between the 1830s and 1880s.

MEN OUTSIDE MARION COUNTY COURTHOUSE. It is not known when this photograph was taken, but circuit court was reported in the *Montgomery Advertiser* on August 22, 1913, as being in session in Hamilton. The Honorable William Brockman Bankhead, candidate for congress, addressed voters who were present, as did the Honorable W. D. Sead and the Honorable John H. Wallace, both candidates for governor. It was reported that all made good speeches, and the people were highly pleased.

AUNT KATE CHILDERS. Aunt Kate, pictured here, reveals and affirms the pioneer spirit possessed by those gone before. The determination that she can and will overcome, that she will prevail, is so evident in her face. Aunt Kate lived near Bull Mountain Creek in northwest Marion County. In the late 1800s, the Bull Mountain community had a community store, cotton gin, gristmill, flour mill, carding factory, blacksmith shop, a kiln for making pottery, and a post office. There was also a combination church and school. Today there is little evidence of the days gone by.

FORD CARAVAN VISITS WINFIELD. History records that on April 14, 1931, Henry Ford and son Edsel drove the 20 millionth Ford off the assembly line. "Twenty Millionth" was painted on both sides of the car and on top. Ford took the car on a nationwide publicity tour. A caravan of about 20 cars visited state capitals and small towns. This photograph was taken when the 20 millionth Ford caravan visited Winfield.

CROWD SHOWS FOR FORD'S CARAVAN. Many people turned out for the 20 millionth Ford caravan's visit to Winfield. A photographer was along, and pictures were taken at every stop. Winfield's photograph had to be taken in two parts because of the number of people that showed up. Schoolchildren were let out of school to see the caravan. It was like a car show and parade.

MARY PEELER LITTLETON REESE. In 1920, she was left a widow with two small children. In 1923, she became director of Marion County Banking Company and served for 55 years on the loan committee and as a vice president for many years. She married Calhon L. Reese in 1923 and later had two other children. She taught and demanded much from her children, but these three demands were most unusual: Never turn anyone away from the door, they have a need or they would not have come; never repeat anything heard at home; and never go in mother's purse. During the Depression, she sold Alabama Power Stock, other utilities stock, and cashed savings in to provide work for hundreds of desperate families. She would get up before dawn to drive a pickup truck of farmhands to the fields to pick, pack, and ship strawberries. Mary Reese was truly a woman ahead of her time.

Visit us at
arcadiapublishing.com

www.ingramcontent.com/pod-product-compliance
Lightning Source LLC
Chambersburg PA
CBHW050653110426
42813CB00007B/2004